Common Tongue

Fraser Scott

methuen | drama

LONDON • NEW YORK • OXFORD • NEW DELHI • SYDNEY

METHUEN DRAMA
Bloomsbury Publishing Plc, 50 Bedford Square, London, WC1B 3DP, UK
Bloomsbury Publishing Inc, 1359 Broadway, New York, NY 10018, USA
Bloomsbury Publishing Ireland, 29 Earlsfort Terrace, Dublin 2,
D02 AY28, Ireland

BLOOMSBURY, METHUEN DRAMA and the Methuen
Drama logo are trademarks of Bloomsbury Publishing Plc.

First published in Great Britain 2025

Cover Photography by Josie Morrison Young

Graphic Design by Robyn Black

A catalogue record for this book is available from the British Library.

Library of Congress Control Number: 2025945592

ISBN: PB: 978-1-3506-0460-5
ePDF: 978-1-3506-0461-2
eBook: 978-1-3506-0462-9

Series: Modern Plays

Typeset by Mark Heslington Ltd, Scarborough, North Yorkshire

For product safety related questions contact
productsafety@bloomsbury.com.

To find out more about our authors and books visit
www.bloomsbury.com and sign up for our newsletters.

Common Tongue

By Fraser Scott

Common Tongue was first performed at the Lanternhouse Theatre, Cumbernauld in September 2024, with the following team:

Bonnie	Olivia Caw
Writer/Director	Fraser Scott
Producer	Jennifer Galt
Set & Costume Design	Mela Adela
Lighting Design	Benny Goodman
Sound Design & Composition	Patricia Panther
Stage Manager	Indi Kilbride

It subsequently toured Scotland in autumn 2025. *Common Tongue* was produced by JGProducing, in association with The Gaiety.

The production was supported by Creative Scotland's Open Fund for Individuals.

Content warning: Strong/explicit language.

Fraser Scott is a director and playwright from Paisley. He studied MFA Theatre Directing at Birkbeck, University of London, where he was supported by the Andrew Lloyd Webber Foundation and the Cross Trust. Fraser was the Resident Assistant Director at the Octagon Theatre from 2024–2025.

Previous directing work include: *Athens of the North* (Scottish Storytelling Centre); *The Gray Plays* (Òran Mór) and *CRISIS: A Rallying Cry* (Traverse Theatre).

Common Tongue is his debut play.

Olivia Caw is a proudly working-class actor born and bred in sunny Cumbernauld.

Graduating from East 15 Acting School, Olivia went on to perform in Scandinavia with Street Theatre duo Cocoloco (2019), later joining the cast of *Trainspotting Live* (2022, 2023).

Olivia has narrated two audiobooks (*How to Survive Everything* by Ewan Morrison, *Santa Steals Christmas* by Eve Nairn Magnete). In August 2025, Paul Sng's documentary *Irvine Welsh: Reality is Not Enough* will premiere at the Edinburgh Film Festival and Olivia's voice will be heavily featured alongside one of her biggest inspirations, Maxine Peake, as well as Stephen Graham and more.

With thanks to

Angus Taylor, Leyla Josephine, Peter Arnott, Braw Clan and Rob Willoughby for helping get the play to where it is now.

The Gaiety, Cumbernauld Theatre, Platform Glasgow, Creative Scotland, Playwright Studio Scotland and Paisley Book Festival for giving the play space, time and support.

And to Olivia Caw and Jennifer Galt. This play would not exist without you.

alas poor country almost afraid to know itself

Common Tongue

A play fur wan actor

Statement of Intent

In the moments before, we hear everything at once: playgrounds, dinners, rain, fireworks, parties, life. Building to:

Bonnie *onstage, surrounded by microphones like some kind of all-encompassing press conference.*

The hum of feedback pierces the silence.

Bonnie   Awrite.

It's funny how sometimes you staun up tae speak and you've got nae idea whit's gonnae come oot yer mooth.

No driven by yer heid, but lit . . .

Something deeper.

A subconscious you that's talking fur ye. Lit you just say something aun you cannae understaun where it's came fae or why you've said it

See it's got me in a a bit of bother. No serious mind you, just lit –

Aye.

A forgot tae pay a parking ticket right, cos of lit, family stuff. It wis sat under a pile of other shite, a totally forgets aboot it aun then a end up wae a letter through the door fur a fuckin court summons.

Imagine me pure in the dock fur a parking ticket.

A hudnae done anything wrang really, aun suddenly there's this judge pure staring me doon fae up on high gi'ing me lip wi Bonnie McKay this aun Bonnie McKay that.

Anyways a pit ma foot in it didn't a?

Runnin ma mooth, yet again.

A dinnae want yous tae misunderstaun but, cos a pure love talking, but folk dinnae awys love listening, aun av heard how a sound, so tae be honest a can see why.

But it's easy tae forgot that bit. The listening bit. Aun a hink it's great listening tae folk. Aw the wee nuances in how they speak. The disagreements aboot whether it's a dressing goon oar a hoose coat, aun if you've been cawing it a dressing goon yer hale life, and then yer mate caws it a hoose coat, suddenly that like –

Changes yer perception of this person. They're no the person you thought they were. You thought they were your pal, but actually they caw it a hoose coat so they must be an entitled prick.

Am sure a just seen somdbdy get a wee side eye there at me mentioning that.

I cannae see yous very well.

Could we maybe – how's aboot we have a bit mare light,

So a can see yous aw?

Lights come up.

Aw, look at you lot. Stunners.

I'll just get on wae it then.

Where wis a?

Aye. Talking.

Talking wi'oot hinking.

Something a am very fond a dain.

When a wis wee ad get it fae teachers and that.

> Bonnie McKay, think before you speak next time.

Oar

> Bonnie McKay, you could talk fur Scotland,

Oar,

> Bonnie McKay, gonnae just haud yer wheesht?

A mind in primary, we were dain they solo talks.

We aw hud tae talk aboot somedy that inspired us.

A famous Scottish person.

A hudnae gone yet, but wee Kevin Gillies wis just finishin' his:

Presentations

In school. Primary school.

Bonnie   And that's how Lorraine Kelly is my favourite Scottish person.

> Very good Kevin, excellent work. Round of applause please boys and girls.

We aw clap.

> Right, who's next?

Imagine you hud tae get up, aun talk about somebody you pure loved. A Scottish person.

> Bonnie?

A cannae avoid it anymare, so a start walking towards the front of the class.

Twenty pairs a eyes staring at me,

Twenty laughs being held in,

Sweat drippin doon ma back, intae ma arse crack.

A can feel ma tights sticking tae ma legs.

Av scribbled whit am saying on a scrap of paper, folded up in my haun.

I bring it oot and grip it close tae ma face, aun clear ma throat:

Ma solo talk is oan ma papa who a like very much.

> Speak up please!

Ma solo talk – is oan ma – ma papa. Who a like very much.

> Your papa?

Aye.

> Pardon?

Yes

Now. We did ask for famous Scottish people, didn't we?

Yes.

Is your papa famous?

No

Which is actually a lie, because ma papa is famous at the bowling club for bein an undefeated champion four year running, but a didnae hink that's whit she meant.

So I just stood there.

Carry on then.

My papa has worn the same pair a tortoise shell glasses fur forty years, the same tartan bonnet for thirty, and the same widden walking stick fur the past ten. He lived in Paisley. He still lives in Paisley, three streets doon fae the hoose he grew up in. Wi me.

Ma papa is sixty years old.

He was born in 1946.

He was my age in 1955.

My papa is retired.

He likes golf and reading the newspaper.

He reads a paper that I'm not allowed to look at because it has naked ladies inside it, but a dinnae know how I'm no allowed tae look at the naked ladies if he is.

My papa is a writer as well. No fur a job, he just does it. He reads at Burns suppers sometimes aun he knows all of Tam O' Shanter off by heart.

And he likes tae write wee poems.

This is a poyum that he writ;

When yer born first ye've nae hair at aw'

Jist a wee roon heid lit a baw'

Aun when yer getting auld

Aun yer starting tae get bald

Then yer back tae the place where ye started.

I look aroon at aw the folk in ma class. At ma teacher. Aun they didnae seem tae like the poyum as much as a dae. They didnae seem tae get it.

But a didnae tell my papa that. Cos a liked it. A like everything he writes.

Ma papa was born in 1946.

He grew up in a country wi an industry that wis already in decline.

He loved God, he loved his wife aun he loved his country.

Well, he loved his second wife.

The year he was born, the Scottish Education Authority wrote that Scots 'is not the language of educated people and could not be described as a suitable medium of education or culture'.

A couldnae believe it when he telt me that.

Disneyland

Bonnie *tries to get back on track.*

Bonnie   Anyways. A hink folk probably thought a wis a bit weird at primary school. But a thought they were weird tae. Lit Rachel.

Yeah so like We did a two weeks in Disney, and then a week in Universal, and then Like I went on Space Mountain twenty times and we got McDonald's every day and the McDonald's over there is like so much better than the McDonald's here and stuff.

Whit did you dae over the summer, Bonnie?

Em, me and ma papa went oot fur the day . . .

Went out where?

We went tae this place aun it had like boats and ice cream and like, you could pure go fur a swim in the sea and it was roastin hot and there wis like an arcade and stuff

Oh right. That sounds a bit like Portugal, were you in Portugal?

No.

Cos you've no really got much of a tan. I've got a really good tan my mum says am a wee bronze angel. What wis the place cawed that you went on holiday?

Millport.

Oh I see.

Well, maybe you can go to Disney next year if you're lucky.

A never was lucky, but it's no lit a never asked.

Papa. Papa.

Can we go tae Disneyland?

Rachel said it's dead good,

Aun theres like rides and stuff

Please please please?

And he'd aways say the same hing

Disneyland?

Disnae matter mare lit

He thought it was hilarious.

Ma papa wis never really a saver,

Aun the state pension's no Disneyland money

He wid take me oot fur wee treats but,

He didnae like saying naw

Didnae want me tae feel like a wis missin oot

Or embarrassed

Or unlucky.

Aun the hing is,

Me and Rachel grew up in the same bit, went tae the same school, hud the same pals.

We just lived in hooses that hud different priorities.

Her parents must've hud a passion fur Mickey Moose, aun there's fuck aw wrang wi' that.

Family Dinner

Bonnie   High school wis awys lit that. A melting pot of class and culture, built in the middle of a suburb and a scheme, where a starts hangin' aboot wi' this boy.

He's awfy pretty, awys dresses dead nice aun that.

Chinos, Hollister tap, the works.

A hudnae hud a boyfriend before, partly cos a hink ma papa wid kill me, which is why he dosnae know, aun cos am fifteen and it's exciting tae keep a secret lit a boyfriend.

Wan day ma boyfriend says tae me that am invited roon fur dinner.

Right.

                                                    Is tonight good?.

The night? Aye, that's fine.

Al just come roon at lit –

                                                    Half six

Haulf six.

Cannae wait.

Oh my god.

A hudnae been tae his hoose before

This felt lit a big step.

Like,

We'd obviously been on dates and stuff,

Nando's, medium sauce tae prove am hard.

But a wis gonnae meet his parents

That's lit

Well that's marriage stuff

A take a wee while getting ready – A full valet aun touching up ma Bondi Sands tan fae the night before

Who's a bronze angel now Rachel ya wee bitch?

But a end up getting tae his hoose a wee bit efter hauf six. Closer tae half seven really.

Am chappin oan the door, pure oot a peach, worrying aff started tae sweat ma tan aff already when he opens it.

The bus wis late. Wisnae ma fault. Sorry.

It's cool.

Aye. It's cool. A walk inside. Steppin intae this –

Shoes.

Whit?

Can you take your shoes off?

Oh. Yeah. Sorry.

Shit.

A shoes aff kinda gaff.

A take my gutties aff and they look oot a place here. Like, a imagine trainers in this house don't even look worn, let alane have the soles falling aff them.

A gie ma boyfriend a quick winch hoping he dosnae mind the wee bit a sweat dripping doon ma face, aun a follow him through intae the kitchen.

Pristine, cream carpet shifts intae pristine grey vinyl. It's lit a showroom for the Next Home catalogue, aun a start hinkin that a need tae no sweat ma fake tan all over this boy's good cream cushion

Everyhin's fuckin reflective, or got wee sparkly bits oan it,

There's nae

Personality

Nae photies

Nae dents fae where the TV slipped aff the unit

Nae stains oan the cushions oar unwashed dishes.

One a they

'Everyhin's goat a place

And if it dosnae have a place

It disnae belong in the hoose' types

They types

His maw and da, are in the kitchen cooking dinner.

The'gither.

Am so sorry am late.

    Oh don't worry about it. Lovely to meet you, how are you?

A straighten up, try to cover the wee hole in my sock, quickly warm up my mooth

Not bad. Yourself? Thanks.

        Oh we're good. Would you like a drink?

Have you got any juice?

           We might have orange squash?
            Michael, have we got squash?

No, like, a can of juice. Like coke.

        Oh right. Yes, we'll have a look.

The maw goes intae the fridge and pulls out a big glass bottle full a water and pits it oan the table.

Dae these folk no know it comes oot the tap?

Me aun ma boyfriend sit doon, and the maw and da join us.

It'll just be another ten minutes.

We're aw sat at the table, the four ae us. Aun then the press conference starts.

So, how are you getting on at school?

Good. Well, yeah, whatever, it's fine.

And what do your parents do?

Oh, I live with my papa.

I see. And he's . . .

Retired. He's seventy-five. What do you both do?

Well, Michael is a Marketing and Communications Associate Development Officer, and I am the Head Business Liaison of International Affairs.

Wow, that's . . .

That must be . . .

Wow.

What do you want to do?

Christ alive, av only given this boy a couple a hand jobs aun a feel lit am in fuckin Taggart.

I'm not sure yet. I enjoy English and that.

I always say you don't really learn English until you're out in the real world. They don't teach you how to read contracts in English do they?

Oh shush Michael. What about journalism?

What?

> Have you thought about that? You could make some
> great money, and meet lots of exciting people.

A dinnae understaun journalists.

> Well, their job is to research and interview people,
> and write articles about it in newspapers.

No, a know whit a journalist is. A just mean a dinnae
understand how you can be wan. If a wis a journalist, aun a
wis interviewing a politician or something, a couldnae print
anyhing they said withoot writing liar in brackets after every
quote.

This gets a little chuckle fae the father. He clearly
appreciates a bit of biting political satire.

> Well, what do you like about English?

Just lit, language and that, it's dead interesting, how we talk
aun stuff. But am no interested in other languages. jist
English, which is annoying because they make us pick
another language lit German or French, and a don't wanna
dae them.

> Why don't you want to do French?

Whit am a gone dae wi' French? A just hink it's annoying
that a need tae pick another language when a huv no
interest in going tae –

And I can feel it coming.

I'm trying to think of something.

Tae find the right words.

So a say whit we aw saw when we're stalling in a sentence.

You ken like, huvin a conversation

And it's like,

Yer trying tae hink of something tae say

So you just pit a wee hing tae stall.

It's automatic.

Nae offence intended.

But my mooth makes that familiar fu.

And he looks at me.

He knows.

He gies me a look of lit,

No at the dinner table,

But it's too late.

Am at the 'uck' It's lightning fast.

A huvny even registered the parents starting to flinch in embarrassment.

Yes well I just think it's annoying that a need tae pick another language when a huv no interest in going tae **fucking** France.

Fuck.

Av fucked it.

Ma boyfriend shifts in his seat, he's hit a beamer of course.

The maw looks stunned, as if av just stood up and taken a big steaming shite oan her glass dinner table

The oven starts fucking beeping, cos whitever wis slow cooking in there is clearly fucking done,

Am just, am gonna go tae the toilet

Aun a get up.

Aun find the bathroom.

The downstairs bathroom.

A dinnae need.

A just need

a break.

Aun a know whit's gawn through thier heids.

Bonnie *speaks into the microphone, her voice reverberating around the space.*

> **Where** did you find her then?
>
> I didn't think you'd end up with a girl like **that**?
>
> I mean, so completely **rude**.
>
> Where is she **from**?
>
>
> That's **rough** around there. Bandit country.
>
> Most folk there are **junkies** you know.
>
> I don't want you hanging about with
>
> folk
>
> like
>
> **that**.

A cannae hack this.

Ma boyfriend is still saying fuck all. A boy who telt me that he fancied me, that a wis dead funny, and dead clever, and that he couldn't wait for me tae meet his family cos a will love them and they will love me.

He is silent, the glaikit cunt.

Aun a mean, a dinnae know how else tae fucking . . .

Eccentuate.

A hink tae some folk, tae these folk, they hink am uneducated. Oar angry

Cos if am trying tae say something fucking important, something that a hink matters, then a dinnae want tae get it wrang,

But people are gonnae fucking assume a will get it wrang

Especially people like them. Right?

So it's a fuckin . . .

It dosnae mean am thick, it jist means a want tae say the right thing. Use the right words. Aun am up tae high doe here, reelin in this pristine linoleum bathroom that's never seen so much as a drop a pish in it's life.

So a just open the bathroom door, walk back through the hallway, and straight oot the hoose.

The sound of rain.

It's absolutely lashing outside.

Aun a feel my feet get wet in a puddle,

A realise av left ma fucking shoes in their hoose.

Fuck.

Dreich

Bonnie   I get hame, aun am drippin wet.

Ma papa, reliable as ever, has a towel aun a cup a tea ready
tae go when a get in.

> Yer lookin a bit peely wally there Bonnie.

My god, you cannae be stoating aboot wi'oot any shoes oan,
you'll catch the death!

A dinnae say much.

We dinnae talk aboot that kinda stuff much, aun he disnae
ask me aboot it anyway.

Bonnie *takes off her sodden jacket, and hangs it up.*

We just look oot at the rain.

Eventually

In the quiet

He pipes up wi' a wee poem

One he writ;

> How else do you describe the weather?
>> Say damp, oar wet, oar grey,
> When you can use a wurd like dreich,
>> To tell a dour day

> A hink the weather means alot,
> Tae your average kind of Scot
> Never being too doon trodden
> Even when yer boots are sodden

It's Drookit,

Mochie

Oorlich

Wet

But dinnae be getting too upset

Fur we've got lots a words for weather,

So whether yerr thick

Or whether yer clever,

You huv the language

So ye dinnae haver

Tae describe the weather

When it's dain whitever

Especially when it's pure bucketing

Cunt

Bonnie   A cawed ma high school boyfriend a glaikit cunt a wee minute ago.

Sorry.

Is evdy awright?

A saw some of ye's look a bit

Nervy

A know it's **wan a they words**

No glaikit obviously

Cunt.

A hink it's funny that a word can make somdy so uncomfortable

Regardless of content oar context.

Maybe

Just tae like

Clear the air

We can aw say it the'gither

So we aw feel better

Are yous okay wi' that?

Right.

Here we go.

I'll count down from three.

Aye, we're actually gonnae dae this.

Bonnie *picks up a microphone.*

Three.

Two.

Wan.

CUNT

Music.

The first time a heard cunt wis oan the playgrun'.

Whispered lit a secret 'hing

A bit a bad language

It was a 'dirty' word.

That's whit Jamie Douglas telt me,

The boy that taught me the word

The first time I used cunt

Wis that night,

When a asked ma papa whit it meant

Aun he telt me we dinnae use words that lit in this hoose.

It's no very ladylike

Aun we hate **cunt**

Aun we hate me using **cunt**,

But Jamie Douglas likes when a use **cunt**

It makes aw the boys pure laugh,

Cos a talk lit one a them

Aun cunt makes me laugh tae

Aun it makes me feel good when they laugh,

But then

They say **cunt**

Aun they use **cunt**

Tae talk aboot lassies

Wi' hairy **cunts**,

Oar gaping **cunts**,

Or smelly **cunts**

But it's lit any word

Cos there's a difference between calling ma mates **good cunts**

And Jamie Douglas telling his mates that he

wants my cunt.

Aun **even** if they talked aboot lassies that hud

A hairy flower

Or a gaping fanny

Folk wid still be mare offended

By me calling them **cunts** fur saying that.

University

Bonnie *puts the mic back.*

Bonnie   Sorry. You dinnae want tae hear aboot that. A just find aw that stuff . . .

Interesting.

So a write a fuckin class personal statement aboot it, which gets me intae university, dain an English degree

Plus a thought it wid be nice tae move oot. A didnae want tae live ma whole life in wan place. I'll let Papa huv the hoose tae himsel fur the first time in god knows how long, thanks tae a combination of student loans aun bursaries.

Ma uni is in a different toon. A wee bubble that's apparently in Scotland but feels lit its own wee world entirely. A toon run by old people aun students fae aw over the world.

Am livin wi three lassies; two fae England and wan fae Edinburgh, aun a dinnae ken which is worse.

They all tell me a sound funny, but it's fine cos so dae they. A actually hink a make fun a the East Coast Lassie maire than a dae the other two, explaining tae them that that's a posh bit. That Edinburgh's no as good as Glasgow. But we're aw pals, aun it's nice tae huv pals in a new place.

Every Tuesday morning, av got a class aboot Scottish writing. Am in first year, so we're dain like the history of poetry. Oor lecturer is this classic university man wi glasses aun a beard. He thinks he's dead trendy cos he sits on the desk,

We'll continue looking at our history of Scottish poetry. Let's take a look at one of Burns's seminal works, To A Mouse.

Because Robert Burns is the only Scottish writer tae every exist.

Christopher, would you mind giving it a read?

Christopher is here on he's maw and da's money.

Bearing in mind it's fucking university, he still chooses tae wear a blazer aun tie tae every fuckin lecture.

Christopher is **awys** right.

I close my eyes as he begins reading.

> Wee sleeket, cowrin, tim'rous beastie,

> O, what a panic's in thy breastie!

Aun clearly ma face is tripping me cos the teacher pipes up.

> Is there a problem Miss McKay?

No. Sorry.

I mean, maybe someone else should read it.

> Why can't I read it?

Aun a feel ma papa stewin' fae the other coast, cos he wis. big fan of the guy. Wid speak at Burns Nights aun aw that stuff.

Well, it's – it doesn't sound right. You dinnae speak these words.

And you do? You are speaking to me in English. We all have words that are unique to where we are from. Liverpool has a dialect. Newcastle. Aberdeen. It's not its own language.

> Thank you Christopher. If Bonnie would like to read the poem, then let's let her read.

Eighty pairs a eyes staring at me.

Eighty wee comments being held in.

A clear ma throat. Bring the poyum close tae ma face.

Bonnie *begins to read, in front of the entire room.*

Timidly

Lit a moose.

Wee sleeket, cowrin, tim'rouse beastie

O what a panic's in thy breastie!

Thou need na start awa sae hasty,

Wi' bickering brattle!

I wad be laith to rin an' chase thee,

Wi' murdering prattle!

Aun am starting tae ken now why ma papa learnt the words tae Tam O' Shanter.

It's so he could pit his foot doon aun show aff his language when folk wid laugh at him.

Aun as am speaking, he appears there in front of ma

No ma papa,

But Robert Burns himself.

He's staunin there, wanting me tae keep gawn.

She finds some strength.

Thy wee-bit *housie*, too, in ruin. It's silly wa's the win's are strewin! An' naething, now, to big a new ane, O' foggage green! An' bleak *December's win's* ensuing, Baith snell an' keen!

Aun there's tears rolling doon Rabbie's cheeks, lit a Highland spring. He's alive through me, reading his words, tae these cunts. Am roaming in the gloaming. A feel lit fuckin Braveheart, staunin ower Christopher wae a big fuckin saltire oan ma face. Aun a say tae him

If am speakin English, why dae a consistently huv tae repeat maself, cos you dinnae understaun me?

Aun Rabbie's started scrappin wae Christopher noo. He is so inspired, he's swung wee Chris aroon by the tie and just beating the shite oot a him. It's me aun Rabbie the'gether, aun a just keep going. Keep reading these wurds aun Rabbie keeps punching that prick and ma voice is louder than it's ever been. Aun evdy else in the class gets oan their feet and

cheers and whoops and dyes their hair ginger and starts
dain a Gay Gordons over the desks and Groundskeeper
Wullie appears playing the bagpipes, aun Shrek pours Irn
Bru champagne over the class, and the teacher apologises
tae me, and the government phone me up and say av been
made Makar furever, and they offer me a room in
Edinburgh Castle where a can lay doon how mine will be the
only language in the country and if ye cannae speak it we'll
kick you oot, and a get the whole Tae A Mouse tattoo'ed on
ma back and I become King a Scotland and ma statue in
Glasgow doesnae get a single bit of bird shit oan it.

Bagpipes fade.

Eh

That didnae happen.

A just let him read it in his stupid accent.

Ad prolly struggle tae read Tae A Moose anyway.

A dinnae know whit half the words mean.

A laugh wi' ma flatmate fae Edinburgh aboot the whole
thing, cos at least she undestauns. The English girls come in,
and a tell them how awful it wis hearing the poem in that
accent.

So what? We can't read it?

No, yous can, it just, disnae sound right. Yous jist don't speak
the language. You sound aw proper aun that. Proper Tory
accents.

We're not Tories?

You wouldnae know fae yer accents but

It's not our fault we sound like this.

A know, but, it is a shame.

If we said that to you you'd be furious. You make fun of us.
Not just how we sound, but what we say. I feel like I wouldn't

be welcome in Glasgow. Like, everyone would make fun of
me, or that people would hear my accent and make a
judgement.

Aye but . . .

You say you want people to let you speak how you want to
speak, but that has to go both ways. You have to be okay with
how we sound too.

But the difference is –

You can't say our accents make us sound posh, and then get
angry when people say yours makes you sound thick.

And there is a difference.

Because Scots, like Gaelic, like Doric,

Is awys oan the brink of being wiped oot.

Hus actually been *banned*

Unlike English.

All devouring,

Pronouncing,

Anglicising

English.

But I suppose she hud a point. Because, maybe, me makin
fun of Edinburgh accents is self-criticising, it's dain other
folks' jobs for them, aun actually, me making fun a English
accents is shite, cos av just been talking shite about how
important it is tae be proud of how you speak.

Aun Christopher is right as well. Cos a don't speak like that
poem.

But a dinnae say that. A don't say a word. A just nod in
silence like a good Scot shud.

America

Bonnie You get tae dae a year abroad at uni.

A wisnae gonna go, but ma papa insists.

> Ye huv tae broaden yer horizons, bonnie lass
>
> Plus ye might meet a rich handsome American boy
>
> Aun we can aw move tae Miami

Aun a don't know whit he's talking aboot, cos he's never gone further than fuckin Fort William his whole life,

But a go.

The first of my family tae cross the pond.

Or so a thought.

Into a microphone:

> Oh my god. McKay? My family used to be McKays!
> That's crazy! I'm actually part Scotch you know.
> Do you know a Steven McKay?

Incidentally, a do know a Steven McKay, aun he's enough ae a roaster that he's probably best pals wi' this lassie.

Am here in a place that is definitely no Scotland, but feels weirdly familiar. Lit, we've seen so much of it fae telly aun films that it disnae feel lit a strange place tae be. Ye understaun the jokes. Ye recognise the shoaps.

It's actually exciting, meeting new people and learning aboot new hings.

A huv a chance here tae change everything. I can be a new person in a new world. So a do ma best tae fit in. No be too much. Efter aw, apparently the only cultural context they have of Scotland is fucking *Outlander*, a programme I have literally never seen. A don't even know whit channel it's oan.

But a manage fine. Just keep ma head doon.

No talk too much.

Aun before a know it it's Christmas. A barely hud enough money tae get here, so a definitely cannae afford tae fly hame for two weeks so a jist stay. Av made a friend that looks efter me over the break, aun we end up at some Hogmanay gaff.

There's no Jackie Bird, but it's nice tae be around folk.

Apart fae the conversations a huv wi' people when they realise that am Scottish. Or a huv tae clarify that am no Irish.

Aun sometimes a miss things. Tonight a miss hings.

Miss no huvin tae talk slow.

A miss folk bein able tae tak a slaggin,

Oar bein able tae get a square sausage.

Here, ye tell folk yer away tae get the messages

Aun they look at ye wi' blank faces

Here, where yer fae suddenly become the closest city

Aun yer toon becomes a haun wave,

'Just ootside of'

Wee

There's this American boy I've been chatting to for a wee while at this party

He's askin me a lot of questions.

Bonnie *takes a microphone into her hands:*

>   So like, it's rough right? Glasgow.

Yeah a mean, it really depends what bit you're at. Not really.

>   I love that. That's so funny. Say more Scottish stuff.

Eh . . . like what sort of stuff?

                Just like, Scottish stuff. Everything sounds
                      so funny in your accent. Say haggis.

I'm not . . . Haggis.

                    That's so good. I love that accent on you.

And I realise now that I'm tied to this,

Mocked

Clumsy

Untidy voice

I am always associated with these assumptions,

They talk to me and think I've packed my kilt

                        Accents really turn me on.

Right.

                    Maybe you should say my name.

Eh a hink it's almost the bells

                            The what?

The bells? Lit – Midnight. Almost midnight.

A slip away, back intae the living room tae find evdy crowded
roon the telly, drinks in hand.

They are counting doon.

A couple of them turn tae me, and invite me intae the mix,
aun a see they are aw in a circle, aun they start singin.

Bonnie *starts humming Auld Lang Syne. It loops underneath.*

It's embarrassing

Obviously

I cringe at them butchering it a bit,

But I still join in,

Aun for a moment

It's like am home.

Across a big pond, but still. Here are folk, ringing in the new year wi' a song fae where am fae, in a way that a speak.

Aun a realise that, right noo, evdy is dain that.

A dinnae just feel connected tae Jackie, tae Paisley, tae Scotland, a feel connected tae evdy.

For three minutes, every single year, everyone that rings in the New Year sings a bit a Scots. And that is fucking magic.

What does it mean?

Sorry?

You're Scottish right. I've always wondered. What does Old Long Zine mean?

Em.

It's like, Gaelic, right?

Gaelic?

No. It's just, lit. Em . . .

I don't know what it means.

This song.

These words.

Words that we sing every year. Words that represent our country. Words that we huv shared wi' the world, aun a dinnae ken whit they mean.

Auld is old. A know that.

But, how do we no know?

How are we no telt?

A dinnae ken. I don't know.

A stumble oot intae the night, and it's weirdly warm

Aun a miss the biting cold winter nights where you can see yer breath in front of ye

Aun a ring ma papa

A dinnae know whit time it is back hame

But he picks up

He always picks up

> Hullo Bonnie, whit's up?

What does it mean?

> Whit are ye oan aboot?

What does auld lang syne mean? They're asking me aun a don't know.

A can hear him laughing, which makes me more upset

> Times lang past darlin'. Times lang past.
>
> How are they asking ye?

Times lang past?

But a don't want tae toast the past

Aun they love askin questions lit that

As if am meant tae speak for the whole country

As if am meant tae know

Well, you're oor representative o'er there Bonnie lass

They need someone lit you tae tell them how it is.

You need tae set them straight. That's your job

And he's right. Cos he's always right.

A huv to set them straight because someone has to.

They're awys getting it wrang

They were dain it wrang a minute ago

Auld Lang Syne

They weren't holding hands right.

Aun if a dinna tell them, who will?

A down the drink in ma hand, and march back inside, past all the folk cheersing and winching, tae the American boy that a wis chatting tae.

A wilnae jist say haggis fur ye, but all teach ye actual Scots if ye want

We huv a word cawed stramash, which means a big fuckin argument

Aun we huv a word cawed numpty, which means an idiot, like you

Aun he wis clearly impressed, but a hud bigger pizza tae fry

Awright everyone, listen up.

I am a bit drunk, and I am Scottish, and I am a bit drunk.

And we are going to do this song again.

And we are going to do it

Fucking

Properly.

We are all going to take hands.

Like –

Like this.

Bonnie *demonstrates by herself.*

You three dae it!

She points at the audience, who hopefully take the cue tae link arms

Magic

That's great.

When we aw sing

Aun here's a HAUN

That's HAND.

That's when yous take hauns, no sooner!

Awrite.

Here we go.

A wee practice

Aun there's a HAUN

Everyone, let's go!

My trusty fiere!

And gie's a haun o thine

We'll tak a right gude-willie-waught

Fur auld lang syne

The audience should sing along:

For auld lang syne my dear

Fur auld lang syne

We'll tak a cup of kindness yet

For

Auld

Lang

Syne!

Fireworks go aff.

Hings changed efter that night.

Because actually a wis unique.

There wis nobody that spoke lit me, said words lit me

A got the Americans using words lit wee, oar hingiwe, oar coorie

They loved it. They felt connected tae somewhere they'd never even been

Aun they wereny actually laughin at me. They were never laughing *at* me

They jist wanted to know more about me

And people asking questions and caring about where you were from was class.

They fucking loved me

I saw things I'd never see at home. I learned about writers and poets

About this guy who had written like a hundred books about language.

He has this theory that every language has the same rules and foundations, every language has a way to ask a question, to say something is positive or negative, in the past or present

It's just the order of letters themselves that are different.

In other words, a child's environment determines which language they will use, but they are born with the tools to learn any language effectively.

Before I graduated

I had to write an dissertation.

I titled it

'The Use of Scots At Home and Abroad'

And a fuckin got pult up fur using the word 'outwith' in the abstract

                              But it's a word.

My papa doesn't quite understand.

I know, but they don't have it anywhere else

                    Right. So, whit else are ye meant tae say

Outside of,

                         But that's . . . well that's pish

I know

                         And whit's this essay about?

Etymology. And like

How words change

Evolve

When they get passed on

Or written down

      A see. Well that sounds awfy clever fur me Bonnie lass.

And my whole world feels bigger

My horizons are, in fact, expanded

But a year goes fast and before I know it ma suitcase of new books has flown home wi' me, aun ma dissertation sits lamented aun unread on Papa's cabinet.

Home Again

Bonnie   There's something funny about being away from home. It's as if, in your head, the place you came from doesn't exist when you aren't there. As if like, someone just presses pause until your feet are back on home soil.

That's not the cause, obviously.

I'm stood waiting for my first sausage supper back, and there's this voice

Bonnie McKay?

I turn around and there's wee Kevin Gillies stood in the queue. Not primary anymore but a man. With a beard. Very much a life that has not been paused.

Awrite, Bonnie? Long time no see

And I don't really know what to say to Kevin. I'm not sure how much chat he's got, given he's spent his whole life in this town. And I'm really focusing on the menu above the flyers and hoping he just sort of . . .

Fucks off.

Whit he dain wi' yerself noo then?

Fuck.

Eh, I've just finished uni actually. I was in St. Andrews.

Oh right.

And he's clearly not getting the hint that I don't want to talk. And maybe I was romanticising home a bit, because

It all just feels very small.

No for me, that.

Uni's not for everyone.

Naw, St. Andrews. Cannae stand the beach by the way.

I like the fresh air.

West Coast Best Coast Bonnie.

Of course.

Ye speak to anyone fae school much?

No. Not really. Do you?

Aye, actual wee're huvin a wee do the night round Davie's if ye fancy coming? Am sure folk wid be happy tae see ye.

And the thought of that turns my stomach. That after all of this. After moving away. And going further. And being special and clever and admired. That I'd end up at a house party with a group of people I went to high school with.

That there'd be nothing remotely interesting to talk about.

Thank you. No. I can't tonight.

Suit yersel.

Whit ye dain wae yourself noo then? Got a tidy wee job lined up ad imagine?

No, nothing yet. I'm looking.

And he doesn't really reply. As if he's expecting me to say more. But I've not got anything else to say to him.

Well good luck for it.

Kevin takes two huge pizza boxes and a couple of plastic bags of chips.

Look efter yersel Bonnie. West Coast Best Coast mind.

The Theatre

Bonnie   And I am trying to look for a job. Obviously. Living back with Papa feels quite

Claustrophobic.

And he doesn't really go out as much as I remember. There's no bowling club trophy on the shelf from this year. Or last. So I decide to take us both out.

There's a theatre in town putting on a play. It's quite a cool theatre. Sexy even, with big glass windows, and a shiny bar, posters up fur all the shows you don't want to see, written by all the folk you've never heard of.

Tickets are all digital which my papa can't quite get his head around. They scan my phone to let us in

                  Aun are they takin yer information?

They've already got our information. We gave them it to book the tickets.

                  Bloody nonsense.

You want a drink?

        £6 for a beer aun it's no even a pint? Jesus christ.

It's on me.

             Dinnae be daft Bonnie, al get it.

He unfolds a £20 note from his pocket and joins the queue for the bar.

After a while a look up from my phone, and see him standing talking to the bar staff.

Arguing with the bar staff

        Bonnie, this man's says he's no takin ma money

The young man he's been talking to points to a framed sign on the till that says 'CARD ONLY'

> Cashless? How the fuck am a meant tae pay for ma drink then?

It's okay Papa, al get it.

> This is good money. A worked hard fur this money, aun your no gonnae fuckin take it?

Papa, please, it's alright. I'm really sorry about this.

I tap my card and he hands me two bottles of beer.

The feeling of regret, of bringing him with me, is starting to slowly sink in.

We mostly avoid the glances from the people behind us and get our seats in the theatre.

Once the play starts I forget about the whole thing though, and so does ma papa, who's laughing along, muttering to himself at points

It's *Romeo and Juliet*, but they've rewritten it to be set in Glasgow.

There's some cringe moments.

Mercutio and Tybalt are neds, of course

The Nurse is like someone from *Still Game*

It's . . . fine

But Papa is completely transfixed.

He's seeing this story fur the first time,

Properly,

The jokes are being told in a way he understands

The voices are familiar

The setting,

And I become sort of okay with the cringe.

I mean, it's not like my papa is stupid, but I think the only time he's ever been to the theatre is at Christmas, where the folk on stage sound like him and you shout out and have sweeties thrown at you.

I'm glad he's enjoying an actual play.

We get to the balcony scene,

Juliet lives in a high flat, it's groundbreaking stuff,

And the tension *is* palpable.

Romeo and Juliet are so close to each other

And

In the quiet

The old man with the bottle of beer next to me pipes up

Gie her a winch son!

Ssshh!

Oh my god

I want this chair to swallow me up whole.

Some people turn around to look at us.

There's a smattering of laughter from a few of the seats,

The actors, clearly surprised, break character a bit, which causes more of the audience to laugh.

But my papa isn't laughing

He's looking at me

Why is he looking at me?

He doesn't really say much for the rest of the play,

And we walk home in near silence.

I'm sorry fur dain tha. That must've embarrassed you.

I've never seen this man apologise in his life.

And not because he's stubborn, but because he never does anything wrong.

And I realise why he looked at me, in the theatre,

Was because I shushed him. That noise came from me

And I didn't realise

It was automatic

It was a reflex

You sound different, you know.

What?

Ever since you came back fae America. Pure posh.

A don't. Fuck off.

Yer pitting it oan now

I hate that he said that

That I speak differently.

I *sound* different.

And I still can't figure out the moment where it changed.

We don't talk about that night,

He doesn't go back to the theatre again.

Pub

Bonnie   He still goes oot tae the pub ever Friday night.

His local is, as you might imagine,

A dark and dingy shithole.

Full of old people that have been sat in the same seats fur centuries

And every Friday night, as he goes for his stick:

> Dae ye want tae come the night Bonnie?
> There's a wee band oan, they're magic.

He knows I won't come, but he aways asks.

Aun I don't know if it's because a feel bad

Or because I'm not really sure what to do with myself these days

But tonight

Alright then. I'll get my shoes.

> As a word a warning, the company is pish

We wander together, through the town,

Past the shuttered up shops, and dog shite, through the big, heavy widden door that grant access to this untouched corner of the world.

The smell immediately takes me back. Lager stained wood, musty carpets aun bags of crisps linger in the air. The puggie machine is going off in the corner,

Someone hoping fur a bit of change.

As soon as we walk in folk are up, chatting, talking to us

To me.

Ma papa has with two pints, aun we grab a spot in the corner.

Everyone is asking me things as if I'm the most important person that's ever stepped foot in this place. Asking where I've been and what I've seen. If America was 'like in the films'.

Aun then, through the chatter, and telly, and glasses against tables

A fiddle pipes up from this wee band hiding in the corner.

Aun everyone goes completely silent

A fiddle plays.

Magic, right enough.

Aun then this old guy from across the bar stands up,

Gripping his pint, clearing his throat.

Aun he's singing alone tae the fiddle.

Singing auld wurds a dinnae know, but a join in on the clapping, aun the shouting.

When the song finishes and there are whistles and cheers,

But the fiddle keeps gawn, picking up speed,

Aun then this other auld yin is up,

So there's this wummin right

Fae Glasgow Right

Aun get this

She's git pure sare teeth, right

Lit

Sookin sweeties every day

So she's goat pure tombstones right

Aun get this right.

So she hus tae get a dentist appointment right

Which is a fuckin nightmare these days by the way

But she manages it

Aun shes in the waiting room right

Aun then she goes intae see the dentist right

And settles doon in the chair right

'Comfy?' asks the dentist.

'Govan,' she replies.

Aun a start looking aroon tae see who's gonnae go up next,
aun the auld man beside me is up

Stood on his chair as if he's twenty year auld.

A wance knew this lassie,

An awfy bonnie girl,

Aun she loved hame an awfy lot

But she also loved the world

Fae day dod, she'd say tae me

Caun we go oot past the sea,

Go oan planes, find new stars

Go tae places near and far,

A cannae go, I said tae her

Ad haud ye back wherever we were

Fur a am auld and you are new,

And this world is reserved for you

Aun so she went

Tae find new faces,

Aun she found new words
In strange new places
Aun soon she spoke
In brand new phrases,
Her auld voice
Only there in traces

Fur it's hard tae hold her ain,
When yer voice is all alane,
It's easy tae be feart tae talk,
Tae let yer roar become a squawk
The lassie used tae speak wi' pride
As sure as the rain, as strong as the tide

But noo she havers, her voice is saft
But shouldnae be feart of sounding daft,
Cos the words she says are mine,
And the words a say are oors

So Bonnie,
Och, Bonnie lass
Aw that a say, An aw that a ask
Is dinnae forget
the hings that last
Words lang gone
Aun times lang past

Abstract

Bonnie   And

He's right

He is always right.

Cos the hing is

It's easy tae tweak how ye speak,

Gaun through phases of rephrases, tensing in wrong tenses,

Deciding whether tae greet or cry,

A dinnae ken where a fit

Cos ma Scots isn't up tae scratch

Aun ma English is pish.

I didn't know that getting out makes it so hard tae come back.

It's no wonder we cringe at the sound of a Scottish voice

When so many of these folk that represent us aren't authentic

Arny real

How can we possibly let a Scot be sincere?

How can yous?

Is that not why am here?

Tae be thick

Dain bits

Aun am the joke

The jock

The jake

The Scot

The Scotch

Perpetually rained on

Shat on

Spat on

And actually,

We let it happen

Av done it tae myself

Tae evdy

Laughing at folk being fae Edinburgh, oar England.

Changing how a speak.

Letting myself no be maself

Telling ourselves and each other that we're

No Scottish enough, too Scottish, Scottish but posh, Scottish but cringe

Bonnie *takes the mic, pulling the cables out and around the stage.*

But it's exhausting, changing the way a sound,

'to make sure I am understood'.

Forcin ma mooth tae dae mental gymnastics.

Tripping over words that feel foreign spoken this way.

Chippin away at letters tae fit inside yer lugs.

Aye, some folk sound lit me;

The skint, the stupid, the stoater,

How is it possible for someone wi' intellect to speak with nae etiquette?

Ma tongue feels tied like a tie roon ma neck

Badly worn, worn out

Turning ma ayes tae yeses to keep yer eyes on me.

Feeling like a don't belong.

'R's no bein rolled,

'T's scattered round the floor,

Coz I've been drapping them my whole life

Being telt tae to pick them up;

Cos 'that's not speaking properly'

Aun 'we don't want you talking like that'

Bein' diglossic's psychotic when yer switching fae fae tae from when you're speaking to someone fae somewhere that's no where yer from.

But there's a hidden complexity tae oor linguistic dexterity

Using words like cunt and fuck no tae offend, but tae express,

However, a admit some ay us use them tae an excess.

A wis told as a wean that tae access success a hud to speak 'proper' so I wouldnae regress tae a 'bam' oar a 'jake' oar a 'junkie' or 'ned', tae use better letters, better language, instead.

We shouldn't be embarrassed fur how we sound.

Folk who speak 'better' are saying much dafter shite in front a the world,

And naebdy seems tae bother wan bit.

Sounding great but saying nothing.

Underneath all the folds and creases, when the shouting stops and the swearing ceases

We scream over cries to 'sit down' oar 'speak right'

These words that we use are a fucking birthright

Aun there are folk across the country,

Spikkin in different leids wae different accents,

Wi' different words in different ways,

Haudin their ain.

Aun a love listening tae folk

However you sound,

Aw the wee nuances.

How the way we live oor lives changes how we speak.

How the words we use, and the way we say them

Carry the history of oor lives aun the folk in them.

The folk that matter.

So it's no slang.

How a speak's no wrang.

That's all a wanted tae say.

Tae . . . figure oot.

Footnotes

Bonnie   Ma papa passed away recently

In case ye were wondering.

A wis kind of in charge of everything, so it wis –

Aye

Ma papa taught me how tae walk.

Tae read,

Tae write,

It wis jist me aun him

Aun words.

A spoke at the funeral

Read out a few of his poems

Evdy hud a laugh aun a greet.

But a managed tae hold it the-gither.

Oh that was how a got the parking ticket. Mind that?

Fae the council.

A didnae pay it, aun a didnae pay it fur a while

A got distracted by hings

A wis busy efter the funeral

Writing stuff

Aun then a forgot aboot it.

Until a got the court summons

A fuckin court summons over a parking ticket by the way

A wis aw prepared but,

A hud the information fae the funeral
Wis gonnae say a wis grieving and get it aff,
Thank you Papa very much.

When it's ma turn, I'm brought up tae the judge
Who asks;

Are you Bonnie McKay?
Bonnie *holds a microphone close to her face.*
Aye.

The judge sort of shuffles in his seat.

I must insist you answer the question with a yes or no.

Are you indeed Bonnie McKay?

Aye.

The judge leans forward again,

Madam, you will be placed under contempt of court if you
cannot answer yes or no.

Aun it's funny how sometimes you staun up tae speak and
you've got nae idea whit's gonnae come oot yer mooth.
Lit no driven by yer heid, but lit . . .
Something deeper.
A subconscious you that's talking fur ye.

But you know exactly where it's come fae aun why you've said it.

Madam, you will be placed under contempt of court if you cannot answer yes or no.

Do you understand that?

Aye.

Blackout.